Coolmind

'The book *Coolmind* is full of handy hints and in-depth lessons on how to stay calm, relaxed and embrace both life and yourself to the fullest potential ... The book and all its lessons have been invaluable to me and I often find myself doing the exercises without even realising it; they are almost second nature to me. *Coolmind* is written in such a beautifully simple yet highly enjoyable and effective way that students are able to easily read it and put the content into practice.'
— *Lara*

'Stress will become an alien feeling after reading this book!'
— *David*

'Personally I found that the mind work was something that, once learnt, I could apply to all aspects of life. Visualising the moment beforehand made everything that happened in races or even exams expected, even though in reality there's always that degree of uncertainty. And I think it is that sense of control over the uncontrollable that helped me the most.'
— *Laura*

'It would have been pretty awesome to have something like this when I was finishing my exams, not just for myself, but for mates of mine who I knew were stressed out but just couldn't seem to shake it. Thumbs up!'
— *Mikey*

Coolmind

David Keefe

EXISLE
PUBLISHING

First published 2011

Exisle Publishing Limited
'Moonrising', Narone Creek Road, Wollombi, NSW 2325, Australia
P.O. Box 60–490, Titirangi, Auckland 0642, New Zealand
www.exislepublishing.com

A CIP catalogue record for this book is available from the National
Library of Australia.

ISBN 978 1 921497 93 3

Designed by Tracey Gibbs
Illustrations by Tracey Gibbs
Typeset in Adobe Text Pro
Printed in Singapore by KHL Printing Co Pte Ltd

This book uses paper sourced under ISO 14001 guidelines from
well-managed forests and other controlled sources.

10 9 8 7 6 5 4 3 2 1

Disclaimer
While this book is intended as a general information resource
and all care has been taken in compiling the contents, this book
does not take account of individual circumstances and is not in
any way a substitute for medical advice. The techniques included
are not intended to be a replacement for treatment by a qualified
practitioner in instances of mental illness. Neither the author nor
the publisher and their distributors can be held responsible for any
loss, claim or action that may arise from reliance on the information
contained in this book.

CONTENTS

Your teacher is laying out the exam papers in front of you and you're starting to stress. You have only a few minutes to get yourself together before the exam begins ... how do you stay calm?

At a party, someone you're keen on is walking your way. You always seem to get nervous about dating so how do you stay cool and not make a goose of yourself?

Competitors in the final look pretty determined.

They are staring you out. How do you stay focused and rise above it all?

Are you fed up with being nervous and full of self-doubt? Do you wonder how you will ever get to feel confident and comfortable with yourself?

Are you bursting with energy to try something new ... but the same old nerves and doubts freeze you up?

If any of these situations seem familiar to you, then you have found the right little book, because this book is all about the art of relaxing, the art of becoming consciously cool *now* to rise above stress. And the good news is ... it's not hard!

WHAT IS A COOLMIND?

This book is a crash course in getting cool 'n' calm no matter what is going on in your life. You'll find it will take anywhere from just a few minutes to fifteen minutes of practice a day to get a coolmind.

The title 'coolmind' comes from an old saying: 'With a cool mind and a warm heart', which means to act with a clear mind and a passionate heart about the way you want your life to be.

Someone with a coolmind is no stranger to happiness. They are not at the mercy of their moods, not pushing hard against the flow of life and not letting fly with wild emotional displays.

We are all born with a coolmind but somewhere along the bumpy road of childhood we begin to cover it over with worries, fears and concerns. We call this 'conditioning'. Conditioning is what we try to protect ourselves with, but these protective thought patterns stick and then as we climb out of the short pants of childhood into adulthood, they just get in the way. In fact, most of the time they just serve up anxiety and other miserable stuff that keeps us stuck in our drama.

Getting a 'consciously coolmind' is, at least in theory, one of the simplest things in life to do because you don't have to think.

> Stress and anxiety mean that worry thoughts are going through your mind ... a coolmind will help you release these thoughts and let go of any worries.

In fact, it's all about practising the art of *not* thinking — or at least no negative thinking — if only for a few minutes at a time.

If you are wondering how it will ever be possible to 'not think', have you ever noticed the momentary calm when you sneeze? Sneezing stops thought in its tracks, which gives you a glimpse of a quiet mind. It's a calming moment.

Coughing and yawning can have a similar effect.
So does the pre-sleep phase.

> There are two main ways to reduce stress and worry in your life ... practise the habit of moving negative thinking to more logical, positive thoughts, which is not always easy, or practise the art of relaxing your mind with meditation techniques.

So how can relaxation and meditation help me?

Relaxation techniques are basically all about helping you to find your 'neutral' feeling place. This is the place where there's just you and your body, without stress, without the thinking. Your coolmind is a calm place and, importantly, you can find it any time you need to!

To put it simply, the art of relaxing and getting a coolmind lies in learning how to 'let go'. By learning how to let go, you are dropping your 'resistance' to the things causing you stress in life. The more you fight or dramatise the things in your life, the greater the stress you will feel.

> Coolmind is about finding relief in any situation. Finding relief is the essential precondition of calm and happiness.

WHY DO I NEED A COOLMIND?

Stress can come in many forms. Here are a
few ways we bring it on ourselves: thoughts of
being inadequate, thoughts of being unworthy,
thoughts of being ugly, thoughts of being stupid,
thoughts of not being good enough, thoughts
that the world will end if I don't get 95 per cent
in this exam, thoughts that 'they hate me'.

> When you reduce your thoughts, you induce
> relaxation, and when you induce relaxation, you
> reduce your resistance.

When you let go of that sort of thinking, you momentarily drop your resistance to life. That's what happens when you go to sleep; you 'let go', you drop 'resistance'. And that is why sleep feels so good, particularly when you are stressed.

So stressful feelings in the body are really alarm bells telling you that you have resistant thoughts to what is happening in your life. Stress can manifest itself in the body in many different ways, such as in headaches, stomach and digestive problems, back pain, frequent colds, tiredness, difficulty thinking and the inability to make decisions (the 'don't know' mind).

When you think a thought, either good or bad, your body responds with a chemical to let your body 'feel' the thought — it matches the thought to a bodily sensation. If the thought was 'This is a disaster!' your chest might tighten or you might feel sick. If it is a happy thought, your body will feel light and loose. Think a panic thought and your body will create chemicals to make you feel panicky. This is known as the flight or fight response because your chemical system is making adrenaline to help you either stay and fight or take off. In the same way, calm and happy thoughts will make your body produce chemicals that enable you to feel calm and happy. Studies have shown that angry thoughts create a bodily feeling that creates even more anger.

> Stress urgently diverts the energy required to keep your mind and body healthy into flight or fight chemicals, which, over the long term, run your system down.

Anger literally creates more anger. You see lots of live demonstrations of this on the roads.

If anger is the appropriate emotion to help you express something or to make you act when something is just plain wrong, well, go for it. But move through it quickly before you end up staying in an angry space and doing angry things. But if anger is just the usual way you respond to stuff because you feel threatened when no threat really exists, then learning to take a deep breath and letting the anger go might turn your life around.

If you are often a mess with nerves or panic, or feel useless and full of doubts, your thinking has in one way or another taken you to that state. If, in the middle of those feelings, you try to say positive things to yourself that you don't really believe, well, you just won't believe yourself. What will help you though, is to become aware of your unhelpful thoughts through meditation. By doing so, you will soften these resistant thoughts and reduce their power, so that you can gain clarity.

Talk to most adults in their thirties or forties who have been through heavy stress and you'll discover they most probably didn't learn relaxation and meditation techniques until they desperately needed them!

In school and at university, information goes into your head all day long. You have to draw on so many thoughts as you learn in class, then you have to study and cram for exams. All the time you are learning, expanding, learning, expanding. It should be fun and interesting, but all too often it builds anxiety and pressure within you. So the last thing you need to do is to stress about how to think when you are stressed. A coolmind is the opposite: there's *nothing* to think about. You simply learn to slow down thought, relax, and lessen your resistance. Just let life flow. How cool is that!

But won't people walk all over me if I just let go?

Some people think that letting go, or dropping resistance, must mean losing control. They think that you'll become a pushover, but that's not true. Letting go *when you need to* is the key. Knowing when and how to release resistance to a stress is what will give you control.

Letting go is about realising when to let go of the thinking and responses to life that are just causing you tension and worry, such as when you're faced with things you can't really change. If it is an exam that you're worried about, letting go of the stress and then returning to your studies with a clearer mind and a different outlook will empower you.

Trying to find a positive thought once worry has set in is often too hard and requires just more thinking. But taking a few seconds to cool yourself in the face of stress gives you a chance to stay calm and on top of whatever is happening. So meditation is not about dropping off effort or taking things less seriously, it's about chilling out and then reinvesting your energy and efforts in a clearer, happier way.

Take the final year exams, for example. If your heart is set on a particular path and you need certain marks to get yourself into a university course, if the way you think about yourself or your approach to exams is nerve-racking and making you sick, then you are knocking yourself around unnecessarily and making it hard to perform well. You would benefit enormously by letting go of the thinking that trips you up.

You could ...
let go of any
bodily and
mental tension to improve your concentration and circulation ... let go of the thoughts that tell you your result is going to define you as a success or a loser ... let go and trust that your uncluttered mind will provide the intelligence and creativity you want, when you want ... let go and know that

> Letting go doesn't mean losing control; it means gaining freedom!

whatever happens you are all powerful ... let go and allow your body to heal and be healthy and free of tension.

But how can I be calm when there's so much to worry about?

Worrying about something can give it a chance to get bigger. It keeps it alive and keeps the habit of worry alive.

Sometimes creating a drama keeps your 'plight' alive and critical, but it does not offer any relief to the situation. If your worry habit is alive and well, you'll also find there will always be a new worry to replace any you solve! Believe it or not, once you begin to practise the techniques

> Putting relief in the space where stress was is the way to a coolmind.

in this book, you'll find it is harder and takes more energy to stay stressed about something than it does to just let go of the thinking.

Why should I get calm when there is so much to do, so much I have to conquer?

Calm is the birthplace of happiness, the fountain of creativity, the key to your mental library, the cutting edge of invention, the access point to your intuition, the source of joy and good health, and the launching pad of inspired action. You *can* be at peace any time you want and when you are, you'll know what makes you tick, where you want to go and what you want to do. You will act and it will feel just right. Once you can find your coolmind, you will have the tools to keep going beyond your previous limits. You are who you are, and the sooner you are at peace and excited by it, the sooner life will open up.

It often seems that it's the cool kids who take all the risks and have all the adventure. We watch the cool kids out there on the edge while our doubts and fears hold us back. The same thing can happen with learning and exams. When you walk into an exam, you take all the information that is rattling around inside your head and try to 'bring it up' as you answer the questions. But if you are anxious or panicky, those thoughts hijack your ability to locate the right information.

How often are you then in the shower or jogging and, 'bang', you're hit with the answer? You dropped your resistance without realising it and the answer presented itself.

One meditation teacher described the negative voice in our heads as a parrot perched on our shoulder squawking all day long, 'You can't do that, loser! Squawk! You're hopeless! Squawk!' So we will refer to that negative voice that sucks the fun out of life as our parrot. Your parrot will always resist a coolmind.

How much more fun and challenging would exams be if you could approach them with more calm and positive expectations?

Once you begin to feel at home with the techniques in this book, you will begin to have more choices and clarity in how you react to what's going on around you. From clarity and calm spring intuition, creativity, confidence and happiness. From negative emotions spring anxiety, fear, anger, jealousy and other feelings of doom. By practising the techniques you'll be able to cut down on those negative emotions, think about situations that used to be stressful in a more peaceful way, and nurture yourself. You'll be able to look at issues from a higher perspective — a more powerful place.

When your thinking keeps causing you hassles over things that haven't even happened yet, you are 'futuring yourself' negatively. Futuring yourself negatively scares you right out of the present moment. Come back here! It's time to learn to 'de-future' yourself. Having a cooler mind will help 'de-future' you, or at least give you the chance to 'future yourself' more positively. The more we know ourselves and our motivations, the more power and resolve we have to rise through the doubts and achieve whatever it is we want to.

Regardless of what is going on outside you, if you're happy on the inside you're well ahead of the pack.

Many people who don't have internal happiness need to go and get it from somewhere else, usually in a manner that isn't good. You see it in bullies or vandals or in kids who get hammered on booze — they are trying to find happiness outside themselves, while the reality is that there is endless happiness on offer on the inside.

Happiness increases your energy. Happy people radiate energy. You can see it in the eyes and posture of happy people. Negative states of mind, on the other hand, contract your body and pinch off your energy.

Happiness and anxiety cannot exist at the same time.

Being happy isn't complicated. If you've ever been seriously happy or content you know that feeling when you smile like an idiot for no reason. The cool thing to know is that happiness is never far away or something that's always 'over there'. It is right here, right now ... and you can find it. Real happiness, as the Dalai Lama says, 'is built on the foundation of a calm, stable mind'. Meditation puts you on that path.

So what is meditation exactly?

There are countless descriptions of meditation but the easiest way to describe it would be 'focusing the mind'. Other ways to describe it would be contemplation, healing, and quieting the mind. Athletes and musicians enter a state of meditation when performing, while a relaxed gardener tending to a rose bush could be said to be in meditation. So if you have a relaxed mind and are singularly focused, you're meditating.

Science has shown that during meditation the analytical bit of your brain slows down while the creative bit actually speeds up. So if your head is always full of worries or needless thinking, some of these techniques could help you find some deep peace underneath all the mental chatter.

What will I feel during meditation?

It will be totally different for everyone and the same person will have different experiences on any given day, but here are a few examples:

tingling skin, itchiness, a deep feeling of peace, a softening of the muscles, an awareness of slow deep breathing, moving or swaying. You may be more or less aware of any physical symptoms you have. You could begin to feel incredibly powerful, or vulnerable, or even slightly out of control. There might be a calm stillness in your mind that escapes as soon as you notice it. These are all normal feelings.

WHEN SHOULD I PRACTISE MEDITATION?

Just as a sport is practised or algebra is learnt, the art of cool, for most of us, takes a bit of practice. The good news is that you only have to find a minimum of three minutes a day to begin with. You can even clock them up accumulatively if you must: say, one minute before you get up, one at lunchtime and one before

> There's a saying: 'Trees can't grow strong roots in a storm'. So you need to practise the art of relaxation when the weather is good so you can use it when the weather is bad!

you go to bed. But you do need to do it every day and make it a habit to reap the full rewards. And after you have been practising for a while, you'll find it can take only seconds to reduce worry and bodily tension.

Three minutes a session (if it's committed enough!) is just enough to give you a taste of the unlimited benefits that meditation can bring. Three minutes of mental rest a day from your 'parrot' can be a huge relief for a nervous person. Fifteen minutes a day would be nice if you can dedicate the time, but that might be difficult, so three minutes will get you into the game. It might be enough to introduce you to the 'Aha!' factor.

The 'Aha!' factor is when you experience that little moment of realisation or calm, or when you realise you're feeling good in a situation that would previously have stressed you out. Little moments like these are priceless.

In this book are meditations to improve your concentration, ones that will enable you to tune into your intuition, ones to help you heal, ones to give you power, ones to help you just appreciate life more, and ones to help you dream and feel inspired. So if you're ready and keen to try, now is a good time to get started.

What you can gain from meditation:

Creativity

Health

Happiness

Better concentration

Increased decision-making ability

Improved memory

More energy

Friends

Performance

Love

Confidence

Sleep

Peace

Empathy

What you can ditch with meditation:

Excess worry

Anxiety

Bodily tightness

Whinging

Boredom

Confusion

Drama

Self-doubts

Negative self-talk

Self-obsession

HOW DO I PRACTISE MEDITATION?

There is a little bit of work to do on your part. You have to trust in yourself enough to let go, relax and just breathe for a minimum of a few minutes a day.

There is no religion in this book nor anything spiritual that will have you wearing robes or burning incense or practising witchcraft. The techniques I've given are just practical ways to find your coolmind in seconds. Where you go from there is your journey to decide on!

It's important to note that, although they are all slightly different, the techniques I give here all centre around two main things: letting go and breathing!

Some of the techniques are an adaptation of meditations that have served countless people over thousands of years, helping them quieten their minds to wisdom and happiness.

Whatever technique you ultimately decide to pursue, mindfulness will be at the centre of it (we will look at this in more detail, on page 41). When you first begin, you might not even notice that you have slipped into a daydream, so when that happens don't beat up on yourself, just come back to your chosen technique. Getting frustrated with yourself is one of the little speed bumps you might have to get past on your way to cool. Getting frustrated with yourself is your old habit slipping in the back door!

Coolmind is not too heavy on the 'micro' theory of meditation because for one, there is enough study in your life as it is; and two, there are streams of positive research out there on meditation if you want to study it! The best bit of study you could ever do on the benefits of meditation, however, is to practise it and live the benefits. Make yourself the research.

What technique should I do and how do I know which one is best for me?

Unless you are drawn to one technique in particular, try them in numbered order and give each one a go for a few days, to see how you are feeling. Some people feel immediate benefits from a particular style, while others take years to feel any benefit. Some meditators who have been at it every day for twenty-five years still feel like beginners, so anything is possible for you.

As we are mainly concerned with feeling good, simply use the method that makes you

The golden rule: if any technique does not feel right for you, stop, and do one that does.

feel the best. Always remember that it's not how well you do at it that's important, but just that you are taking time out to do it. There is no doing well or doing not so well, it's just doing!

A quick word on posture!

As we are energetic beings, get into body positions that help your concentration and circulation. Slumped, lazy or sleepy postures pinch off your energy and have no concentrative benefit. I often say, 'Where your mind goes your body goes'. It means that your thinking can affect your health. It works in reverse too. Good posture is a mark of respect to yourself and it is a good habit when you can bring the best of your posture to each session. So sit comfortably with your spine upright and in its natural shape — it should have the shape of a long 'S'. The neck and shoulders can relax without strain and this will enable your ribs to move freely, allowing your body to breathe as it wants. Any position that requires physical effort will only bring you tension, so keep it natural.

Breathing

All meditation and relaxation programs work around your breath, so no matter what technique you choose, you should start your focus on your breath. But why is this?

The main reason is that your breath is your

most immediate connection to life: it is easy to locate in a hurry; you can feel it, hear it, draw it to certain parts of the body and even see it in winter. If you can't find your breath, staying 'cool' is the least of your problems!

Your breathing rate also settles your heart rate. So if your heart rate is settled *you* will be settled. Deep breathing also keeps the oxygen circulating in your body clean, so it can dispel carbons that accumulate in your system.

Focused breathing settles your emotions which in turn reduces the stress chemicals in your body, which settles your emotions further, and on it goes ... So while you could say that 'breathing relaxes my body', you could also say 'an absence of breath causes me tension'!

Concentrating on your breath gives you a quick snapshot of how tight your body is and how busy your head is. During stress your breathing rate may be an erratic one or two breaths a second or you may just be holding it in. In deep calm, you may only take a breath every ten to twenty seconds.

How to work the breath

When you first start meditating, your breath is the leader, not your mind, so all you need to focus on is letting your breath settle into whatever rhythm feels right. Give yourself the time and permission to relax into the rhythm of

You shouldn't force the breath in any way; that only introduces tension.

breathing. Just watch it; be a spectator.

Just feel your body rise and fall with your breath. Think of it like you have just hopped onto the lounge to relax and watch TV. You settle in, get comfortable, and see what comes on. Like your body, you settle down, take a breath, and see what your body and mind are doing right now. Don't go into any thoughts or feelings that you may have, just observe and settle in to your breathing rate as it is.

As the breath settles, the mind can then begin to 'observe' and focus on your chosen technique.

(You can try all the techniques in this book and see what comes most easily to you.)

Try placing your tongue on the roof of your mouth to relax your neck, and if your attention wanders, the next thing you'll realise is that your tongue is on the floor of your mouth. When did that happen?

To breathe most effectively, breathe in and out through the nose and when you feel settled, you're ready to begin your technique.

THE TECHNIQUES

1. Cool mindfulness

Best for:

Concentration

Mental focus

Calming your mind

Quieting your thoughts

Following your breath

I'm sure you have heard it said many times that mindfulness is 'living in the moment'. But while that sounds cute, what does it mean exactly?

Living in the moment means to be fully aware of right now. Your body might be here but where are your thoughts? Most of the time we have thoughts rattling around in our heads about Saturday night, or the exam we're going to flunk — basically, the same sort of thinking that got us stressed in the first place.

As I pointed out earlier, a lot of our stress comes from 'future thinking' — thinking about things that haven't happened yet — particularly when we future think negatively and see ourselves crashing and burning in advance. (If you happen to future think positively, then don't change a thing!)

We need to think ahead about stuff, sure, but a lot of our future thinking causes us worry, so the idea is to try to let go of thinking while we meditate. Mindfulness helps us be more aware of what we're thinking *right now*.

If you are in the habit of futuring yourself negatively, then you are in the habit of rehearsing for things to go badly. But if you see things negatively and they happen negatively, isn't it possible that, if you got in the habit of seeing things positively, that positive outcomes could happen?

Sometimes, rather than finding the right thought to think, it's easier to just go to the breath and notice that the negative thoughts are active. Noticing they are there is the best way to neutralise them, as you can either let them go or try a slightly improved thought.

Try this: close your eyes and think about all the blue things in the room. Then think about all the red things. What were they? That is being mindful. If you came into the room feeling stressed I bet you didn't notice anything. When you are stressing about something you often don't notice the good stuff all around you.

Mindfulness creates a tiny gap between what

happens in life and your response to it. In this little gap is the fruit of self-improvement.

Here's how to do it.

Sit cross-legged on the floor or sit tall in a chair. If you're on the floor, shove a cushion underneath you to take the tension out of your legs.

Let your hands sit freely in your lap, or make a loose fist with each hand and sit them on top of your knees.

Keep your eyes open and gaze at the ground about two feet in front of you — your gaze should be soft, as if you are looking through the floor. If the eye-open method is difficult, then close your eyes but stay as alert to your breath as you can. If you go to sleep easily it might be best to keep them open for a few minutes.

Before you start, give yourself permission to relax your mind and body. You can use phrases on your out breath like, 'letting go ...' or 'I'm letting go easily' or 'releasing thoughts, relaxing the body' or the shorter version, 'release, relax'. As you breathe in you say 'release' and as you breathe out you say 'relax'. These phrases bring attention and respect to the meditation and yourself.

Tip: The words are said silently to yourself, or said very quietly. There is no need to voice them out loud.

As thoughts arise, just notice them, let them go and come back to your breath. The thoughts may seem important but know you can come back to them later. For the next few minutes you have given yourself permission to mentally relax.

With this style of mindfulness meditation, you just concentrate on the feel of the breath, the depth of it, the clearing of the lungs and the softening of the body. Become curious as to how breathing feels, as each breath is unique.

If you are having trouble with a wandering mind, you could try counting your breath, which will give you a focus.

Breathe slowly in through the nose and count your out breaths: 1 ... 2 ... 3 ... 4, then back to 1. You count to 4 and return to 1 so you don't get lost in a game to see how high you can count — that's just another way to get busy!

Another option is to say the word 'two' as you breathe in, as it can soften that empty space between the in and out breath.

You can either just breathe for as long as you feel comfortable — anywhere from a few minutes up to fifteen — or you could set yourself three to five sets of four breaths with a little break in between each set and build your practice up that way.

Once you are relaxed and your breathing is settled, you can also experiment with combining an out breath taking seven seconds with an in breath of five seconds. That way you can set yourself to simply think of nothing else except the breath counts.

A quick word on breath counts: counting for some people can introduce tension to their session, so if you feel that counting introduces tension by making you feel uptight, forget it, let it go and try another style!

Don't force yourself to concentrate, as this brings tension. Just relax, enjoy the fact that your mind is cooling off and keep returning to your breath.

Notes

(Use the space below to make your own notes on how this meditation felt for you. For example, did you enjoy it? Did you find it difficult?)

2. Cool relaxing

Best for:

Calming your mind

Releasing bodily tension

Breathing practice

Letting go

Recovering from activity

If you have physical stress in your body, this is a great technique to help release it. You also have gravity on your side as a bonus!

If your mind is too much of a circus to slow down, work on relaxing your body and the mind will tag along. Remember, where the mind goes the body goes. Here's how to do it:

Lie on the ground with your knees up and feet on the floor (or lie flat if you can stay alert!). Place your hands on the sides of your rib cage in line with the bottom rib and encourage your breath to wander down to where your hands are. You should feel your ribs moving slightly sideways rather than up and down.

As you breathe, do a bodily scan and wherever you find tension just imagine letting it go. Allow it to melt, but if it isn't ready, let it be, relax the rest of your body and check in later.

Say to yourself, 'I can relax easily, it comes naturally'.

Go with it. Let your nerves and muscles unwind and sink into the floor. Let gravity do its thing.

Let your mind just observe your body relaxing.

Your spine will grow heavier as your nerves unravel and tension drains like melting ice.

You can scan your body and relax tension where you find it, or you can begin at the feet and move slowly up your body. Focus on the feet, mentally scan each foot and imagine the tension melting away. Move up through the calf muscles and thighs, make your way to your belly and imagine the stomach walls giving way to calm. Move up through the heart to the neck and isolate the mouth, jaw, eyes and forehead. This should take anywhere from three to twenty minutes depending on your focus and available time. It often helps to flex the muscle you are focusing on and sink into the feeling of it relaxing again.

Or you can try this version:
With your eyes open, imagine peering through

a spot on the ceiling. (That means you gaze at the spot softly like you are looking at something just behind it.) If you must close your eyes, keep the concentration on the breath until you get comfortable, then work through the tension-releasing steps we have just covered.

The phrase 'letting go' is a good thing to repeat a few times as you begin, but avoid saying 'let go' as that can sound like you're barking an order. If you are having trouble relaxing, barking 'LET GO!' will probably end the session right there.

Your body wants to feel energy pumping through it, but it needs to relax and recover. The muscles and nerves in your body need to soften so the tension in your body can dissolve before it builds up. Be aware though, that it's easy for you to drop off to sleep or slip into a daydream if you stay in this meditation for too long, so watch out for that!

Notes

_____

_____

_____

_____

_____

_____

_____

3. Cool visualisations

Best for:

Relaxing

Creativity

Imagination

Empowering yourself

Energising your body

The power you can generate from deep visualisation is unlimited. Fortunately, visualising comes easily to most of us as we spend a stack of our time daydreaming! And if you can daydream, you can visualise ...

You can create anything you want during visualisation so it's a wonderful imagination tool, and it's most effective when you create it as vividly as possible. Liven it up with all the sights, sounds, feelings and sensations that you can imagine until it comes to life within you.

Visualising is a great tool for anything ranging from relaxation to empowering yourself, to healing or preparing yourself for a tough situation. It can be done lying down in a comfortable position or, just as easily, sitting at a desk. Soft music can help to create a good mood for visualising.

When you're ready, just close your eyes, give yourself permission to let go, and see yourself in the perfect environment you want to create. Go as deep into your place of calm as you can and, here is the mindful bit, feel every bit of it — the temperature, the water, the rain, the sun, the mountain mist — and hear every sound: the birds, the waterfalls and the waves.

The aim of this style of meditation is to bring back those feelings of calm or power to what you are doing now. Walk away from each of these sessions with the feelings of how you felt during your visualisation.

Here are some examples that will help you make your own up.

Example 1
You are walking through a rainforest. The sun is splintering through the treetops and the birds are chirping away. You come across a stream and sit on the bank. The morning sun is bright but not too hot, and the dew has just about gone from the grass. As you sit, a fish jumps and splashes near you and the water ring widens across the water. You look closely at the water; what other fish are in there?

Example 2

You are the Almighty, the Creator. You sit on top of your mountain or under your waterfall or float down your river and breathe in the power of it. You are in supreme health and in perfect positive energy. You rejuvenate in your kingdom.

Example 3

Let a time come to mind when someone poured plenty of love or care into you. Go right into it and immerse yourself in the feelings that come up. If nothing comes up or you don't have those memories, make it up or imagine you are doing that for a baby. Imagine how that baby feels. Finish by dropping the thoughts and staying with the bodily feelings.

Example 4

You dive into a stream and the current wants to take you with it. You feel safe so it's no big deal. You start to relax and let it take you. The more you go with it the more you relax and then you realise that the stream is only taking you deeper into paradise. You completely let go and trust the stream completely. As in life, you learn to stop struggling so much.

Example 5

You are on a beach at sunrise and nobody is about. You are doing a few stretches or some yoga, listening to the waves and watching as they sparkle in the sunlight. You start off on a walk and then build speed until it turns into a jog on the sand. You have never felt so light and strong. You are running effortlessly across the sand. Take in the power.

Notes

4. Cool performances

Best for:

Any performance

Concentration

Focus

Rehearsing

Confidence

There is much research to show that the subconscious mind does not know the difference between what is vividly imagined and what is real. If you can imagine it, you can create it. Nervous and panicky thoughts clamp down on our natural talents; they pinch us off and don't allow us to show our best. We end up getting in the way of ourselves. So there is great advantage to be had in mentally rehearsing every bit of a performance you have coming up.

Whether it is a musical piece, speech, gymnastics performance or a rowing final, go through the entire performance in vivid detail, imagining exactly how you want it to go. You will benefit by running through this visualisation as often as you can, well before the performance. Weeks before even. By the time you hit the stage you want to feel like you've done it a thousand times already. You only have to be cool and let your talents do the rest.

So, here's how to go about it:

Get yourself into a comfortable position by either sitting up or lying down. Breathe yourself into relaxation before you begin.

When your mind and body are calm, begin the perfect performance visualisation from the very beginning. Imagine yourself getting ready that morning, confidently and excitedly. Get your bags together. Get to the track or theatre. Feel the perfectly normal tingling up your spine and your energy flowing. Come to the stage or starting line full of concentration and determination. Go through the entire race or act in real time just as you wish it would go.

> Make your performance feel good and always finish while it's feeling good. Don't hang around in there! If anything other than good things appear, don't try too hard to correct them. Just start fresh.

Another great way to overcome any nerves or doubts is to fully understand why you are doing the thing you want to do. If you are feeling nervous about something but know why you are going to do it, you can find great determination in drawing on these reasons.

Do you know why you're doing the thing you do?

Relax for a couple of minutes with some breathing exercises, then ask yourself why you do this sport or activity. Hold the question as an interested spectator and see what comes up. There may be nothing magical in the answer other than that you're trying to have fun, but to know your answer can be very calming. If you come to understand why you play music, train hard, debate, row, etc., you'll always be able to find motivation and a reason to overcome any doubts.

Notes

5. Cool power

Best for:

Empowering yourself

Energising your body

Sport preparation

Getting physically well

Confidence

This is great stuff if you're into feeling more powerful and energised.

The technique is from the Reiki tradition. Reiki is a Japanese word with 'rei' meaning spiritual and 'ki' meaning energy. It is used to enhance the speed of your internal energy for your own sense of wellbeing and available energy.

Begin by sitting comfortably, let your thoughts go and relax into the breath.

Lie down and place your hands across your stomach near the navel. Imagine breathing in a colour, say red, and draw the colour down to your navel where your hands are resting. Imagine the colour giving you much needed energy and strength. With your mind, follow the feelings of energy spreading and filling your body — in through the nose, down through the neck and to your navel, breathing in with the energy and out with the tension. Follow the coloured breath until you are feeling energised but calm.

Use whatever colour comes most easily to you but, as a general guide, reds and oranges are the most energetic colours and white the purest and most versatile. (See page 109 for more information on how to use colours.)

Notes

6. Cool healing

Best for:

Healing

Nurturing

Rejuvenating

Relaxing

To get healthy and stay healthy your body needs circulation. So when we look to heal something in ourselves, we need to relax and let the body do its thing with the natural energy we produce. Your body wants to be healthy and knows how to be healthy if you relax, as health is its natural state.

There are many ways to get your healing process in full swing.

Start by either sitting in one of the meditation poses or lying flat. Allow the body to relax and allow your mind to let go. Place one hand on your belly and the other on your chest so you feel self-supported but also so that you can 'connect' to two of the main energy centres of your body:

the belly and the heart. As you relax, get a sense of the warmth and energy building up around your hands and torso. You can also visualise breathing in an 'energy' of some sort to further enhance your healing energy. The 'energy' could be the colour red from the Earth's centre, a powerful energy from the Universe or make up your own. You can send this energy to the part of your body that needs healing by either giving it your mental attention or by putting your hands on the area.

As you begin to relax, you can also use phrases like 'my body is healing perfectly' or 'my body knows how to heal perfectly'.

If you want to use a visualisation to help heal, it is best to visualise that part of your body already perfectly healed.

Remember: circulation is the key to healing and the key to circulation is being unrestricted in the mind and in the body. So relax and trust that your body knows what to do!

Notes

_____

_____

_____

_____

_____

7. Cool walking

Best for:

Quick mental clearing

Unwinding

De-stressing

Enjoyment

Appreciation

No time to meditate? Try this out.

Walking meditation puts your mind in a cool place pretty quickly, and sometimes this is all the time you're going to get to yourself.

Here's one just made for walking that comes from Thich Nhat Hanh, a Zen monk. While simply walking without any urgency to get to a particular place, deepen the breath and take seven mindful steps in appreciation or gratitude for something in your life.

Take seven steps with full mindfulness and feeling for your ancestors, grandparents or someone recently departed so as to make them still feel part of you. Seven mindful steps are easy to dedicate to someone or something meaningful.

Take seven steps for the air you breathe, your body, the trees, someone who is ill, whatever. Take seven steps for yourself because you're doing pretty well in life.

Breathe with total mindfulness of how each footstep feels. Seriously, how does it feel? How far up your leg does the pressure of each footstep go? Is the pressure through each footstep evenly felt?

Follow the noise of that train until it fades out, listen to the birds or waves and stay with them.

Simply taking in all your surroundings will put your mind at ease.

If you are walking between exams or walking to meet a date, you have done all you can do, so find your cool place in your footsteps by focusing on your technique. The more you can go into your technique, the less your analytical mind will trip you up.

Notes

8. Cool releasing

Best for:

Relaxing

Relieving nerves and stress

Loosening up

Clearing your head

Energising your body

This is a quick-release technique for dumping bodily tension right where you stand. (You can also sit, if you prefer!)

If you're just hanging out while waiting for a performance or the start gun, if you're waiting outside the interview room or have nervously pushed the doorbell to pick up your date, do this technique to quickly reduce bodily tension, to help you chill a little and to think more clearly.

Close your eyes or leave them open, whichever you prefer, and imagine a wave of energy. This energy can be in the form of a colour, a light or a cloud. It starts at your head and moves slowly down your body (how slowly depends on how much time you've got, but the slower the better!), and as it passes through it melts the tension around your head down into your neck and towards your feet.

The wave then comes back up to your head and passes down again. Each time the tension should melt to a lower level in your body until there is an imagined pile of stress and tension left on the floor as you walk away.

Always make sure that the tension goes down through your feet and not up through your head. You don't want to make the mistake of pushing tension into your head until your brain hurts! You also don't want to be interrupted halfway

through and be left with a head full of stress.
Melting or dissolving downwards is the way to
lose the tension.

Practise this anywhere, anytime. You can even
do it several times during the day as a way of
observing how tense you are.

Notes

9. Cool focusing

Best for:

A quick de-stress

Relaxing

Concentration

Noise is a very handy thing to meditate on, so don't treat it as an irritation if it turns up halfway through your session, particularly if it is the sound of rain, which is possibly the best sound of all. Instead, use noise as a tool to help you improve your ability to focus. Noises from fans and fridges, in particular, are actually very consistent so they are easy to meditate to — turn them into a positive.

Another way to use noise to help in your practice of mindfulness is to sit with your eyes closed and try to follow a sound until it fades completely. Follow the train until the noise fades. Listen to a bird's song until it moves away.

Alternatively, sit and concentrate on how many different people's voices you can hear, or how many bird noises are around you. If you're feeling nervous or are waiting for something to begin, it can be very calming to close your eyes, take a few breaths and focus on the noises around you. How many different people's voices can you hear? How many bird calls can you pick up?

After a while, you should be comfortable relaxing to the sound of barking dogs!

This technique can also be used with sight. Instead of closing your eyes and focusing on a sound, watch a surfer catch a wave and ride it right into shore or watch a bird fly until it disappears.

You could also use sight to focus with feeling. Take an object — a tennis ball, a jumper or a piece of fruit — and place it on the floor just in front of you.

Gaze softly at the object and begin to feel it, just as if you were holding it. Turn it around, squeeze it, catch it, feel the weight of it and its texture. Stay focused on the object for as long as you can. You can also consider the life of the object. How many hands has it been through? Who made it? What was their story?

If you don't have an object, think of one and stay with it for three to five minutes. Keep a tennis ball firmly in mind and watch it wherever it mentally goes.

Notes

10. Cool gratitude

Best for:

Feeling happier about your situation

Feeling appreciative

Feeling loved

Developing
compassion

Make yourself comfortable and begin to focus on the breath. Once you have relaxed, turn your attention to things you can feel appreciation for or gratitude towards. For example, you might feel appreciation for a teacher or relative who has pitched in for you recently, or for a gift you might have received, or for something as simple and abundant as the sunshine.

It might sound corny, but meditations on these sorts of positive things can give you an enormous lift.

Appreciation is just a great way to start and finish the day. It feels good and being around appreciative people is energising. If you do it before bed, there's a good chance you'll kick off your day in this frame of mind as well.

Notes

EXTRA STUFF

In case of an emergency

In all cases of sudden stress, the breath is always the first place to check into while you settle down a little. Here are a few other suggestions for handling stressful situations.

Example 1
If you're in a situation where it feels like the sky is falling in or you're under threat, firstly put some space between you and the 'thing', close your eyes and take a few deep breaths. Let the breath

run in and out at exactly the speed it wants to. Let it slow down at its own rate.

If you have a second to do so, check in with yourself. 'Hi nerves, I've got you, it's cool', or similar words, can help you to get some calm back.

Naming the feelings — 'I'm feeling nervous' or 'There is fear going on here' — can help you to settle down. Stick with words that describe your 'feelings' rather than branding *yourself* with another label.

Go to your preferred technique (this is where it pays to have practised!), knowing you have a place of cool. You can also place your hand on your forehead and with your thumb and middle finger press above each eyebrow — these are the ESR points (emotional stress release points) and applying pressure to these points is a reflex way of relieving stress. (You may have noticed before that people often put their palms on their foreheads when under stress.)

Example 2
The speech or performance you were dreading has come. You're walking up to the stage; there is no escape and all you want to do is run.

A golden rule in a stressful situation is to meet the feelings with your breath. Always go to the breath in any challenging situation. Trust that things will turn out as they turn out, and that you're more than capable of handling that.

It is in these challenging situations that you get the chance to really grow. These are the best times to practise being in control, to trust your natural talent. The more you do that, the stronger your self-belief will become. It will take many attempts before you begin to feel more comfortable, so be cool with yourself if the first few don't work out so well. If your self-belief doesn't come up to the mark, that's okay. Your coolmind is happy regardless.

The breath is the gateway to your coolmind. A few breaths will keep the stress chemicals from producing in your body and enable you to trust yourself. Basically, focusing on your breathing will help you to get out of your own way. Have you ever surprised yourself by doing something awesome and saying, 'Wow, I didn't know I could do that!' That's because you were out of your own way and happily focused on the task at hand. The possibilities are endless if we follow our gut feelings and get out of our own way!

Example 3

Things have gone horribly wrong, you're shaking and feeling like you could puke.

When a situation hits you forcefully, do whatever you can right now to feel better. Breathe, use the ESR points on your forehead (see page 96), clear out, take a quick walk, move around, do whatever cuts you some relief.

There's nothing to figure out at this point as your head has probably caved in already. However, know that the 'mind' that reacted strongly isn't the same 'mind' that will figure it out. In the meantime, just try to feel physically better as soon as possible.

It's handy to know that, if you've been practising this stuff, there is a place of calm within you when you need it. If these situations happen often, the fear of freaking out can become greater than the fear of the situation itself. So knowing that you can restore your cool through meditation is your ticket to start taking on those fears little by little.

Talk to someone or get help as soon as you can, because letting high-stress events swirl around in your head just builds the pressure.

Example 4

'Oh no, here he/she is, walking over to me! I should ask him/her out.'

And then the head talk starts, usually badly ...

'I can't ask her out, I'm a moron.'
'I'm a total nerd and ugly too.'

'She'll laugh at me.'

If the head talk is negative like this, just keep saying, 'So what!' to yourself. There's no need to say anything more complex than 'So what!'

'I can't ask her out, I'm a moron.'
'So what!'
'I'm a total nerd and ugly too.'
'So what!'
'She'll laugh at me.'
'So what!'

She or he is probably more nervous than you are anyway, but you don't need to tell yourself that. 'So what!' will do.

Keep saying it until you let go and do the thing you want to do with a 'So what!' attitude. This works for just about any challenge you might find yourself in. It puts the fears back in their place with a bit of comic relief. We often take ourselves a bit too seriously, so this helps to clear the way.

Example 5

Imagine a situation that you are really not looking forward to. Visualise it in all its ugliness. Play it out and then drop the thoughts and see how the situation feels to you — not that great?

Now play it out positively and see how it feels. Better? That's how your life wants it to play out. Take that natural feeling into the situation and watch what happens.

If you are heading home one day and you know there is a hassle awaiting you that you have to deal with, practise the positive visualisation beforehand. Then take that feeling and mood into that situation and be patient with the outcome. If you present yourself to the situation with a more positive attitude, you will create an atmosphere where things may have a better chance of working out for you.

Hurdles!

Your parrot

'I can't do it. I'm just no good at it!' That would be your parrot getting at you before you give yourself a chance. If this happens, just give yourself credit for taking a few minutes out and for noticing that your mind is racing and unsettled. It's normal. Be gentle, relax with the feeling that your mind is off racing and just watch. That's the best way to start.

Your parrot has probably been happily running the show for some years and enjoyed getting you into all sorts of states, so don't expect it to take too kindly to being zipped up. It will have all the excuses: 'I'm too tired. It's dumb. I don't need this. I've got better things to do, etc. etc.' Just be aware of your parrot kicking in with this sort of complaining and bring it along anyway.

The nay-sayers

In the early stages of practice don't talk too much about your meditation unless there are people close to you who you want to share it with. If you talk too much, you can be sure that there'll be someone who wants to shoot you back down to where you were. And if you're gaining benefits from your practice, the last thing you'll want is someone squashing your cloud.

The worrying mind

This is when you always think you have to figure something out. You sit down to relax, then on comes your mind obsessing about something. It can be useful to realise that this type of thinking creates the stress in the first place! It is great practice to recognise unhelpful thinking and know that by putting it on hold while you relax you can help break the habit.

Your phone

It's a good idea to lose the phone or turn it to silent and put it where you can't see it. It's great practice to turn it off even when you're expecting a call. People will leave a message or ring back.

No time to meditate

Sorry, that's your parrot talking! Remember there is a technique to fit any situation, no matter how tight for time you are.

Procrastinating

You have some heavy problems to sort out and you will start meditating when that's done. Oh no! The best time to practise *is* when you feel you're in deep! It's when you can practise feeling calm *during* times of stress that you know you've made a leap forward. When you see through that one, you're well on your way to calm.

Unrealistic expectations

Be patient and realistic. Don't expect rainbows or angels to appear after a few attempts! Cool will flow slowly into your life as your practice deepens ... and it will surprise you when it does.

I can't find a quiet place!

Remember there is a technique for anywhere and anytime. Begin with a couple of techniques and do them walking, in the shower or whenever you can grab a few seconds on your own.

I've had some real growth and I don't get worried anymore!

There is always a new challenge in life and there

will always be room for personal growth. Keep in mind that you will have to expand to keep up with yourself! There is always a place for meditation and dependable calm in your life.

Cool accessories

Working with colours

This might sound bizarre but colours have an electromagnetic quality to them, which we respond to unknowingly. Think about how the colours of things affect you: the colour of your bedroom, your sports colours, your clothing colours. Do people say you look good in red but black doesn't suit you?

Here is a quick look at some colours and how they might affect you if you wear them or are surrounded by them.

Blue

This is a calming colour for the emotions and is known to be inspiring and spiritual. It is also endless and vast — think blue sky or the ocean. If you are often fired up or have trouble relaxing you might need some blue around you.

Green

The colour of nature and growth, green is good for getting well and calming the nerves. Think rainforests, green grass and gardens.

Black

This is a deep colour which has the energy of mystery. It's deep and thoughtful, creative but not big in the fun and calm states.

Yellow

Yellow is light-hearted, easy to see and full of happy, expressive energy. It is good for energising and expressing yourself. Think morning sun and banana energy.

Orange

Orange is great for energising and powering up. It will make your appetite kick in and is good for creativity. Think fresh oranges and long afternoon sun.

Brown

Brown is a solid colour that reflects the earth. 'Grounded' and more serious people get into brown. It's not great for your sense of humour but it will get your feet on the ground if you live in dreamland. Think soil.

Grey

Grey is a mature colour, is neutral and good for thinking. It is not overly energising but good for time alone. Think calming rain clouds.

White

The colour of purity, white is clean and godly. It is great for mental clarity but easily destroyed by beetroot! Think heavenly or puffy clouds.

Red

Red is the most energetic and fiery of colours. It won't help you to sleep too well, but it will help shake off your blues. Think fire and convertible cars.

A final word

The calm was always there, always within, but you can't read about it to know it. Nobody can tell you about it, it's like the taste of an apple ... you don't get to savour it by reading about it. You have to experience calm within you to know it!

So, over to you ...

INDEX